MW01622993

KROKO
VERLAG

Dear reader,

Thank you for choosing our book and we hope that you enjoyed it as much as we enjoyed creating it! Your feedback is very important to us, and we would love to hear your thoughts on the book. If you have a moment, please leave a review on Amazon to share your experience with other potential readers. Your review will help us to improve our work and create even better books in the future.

To write a review simply scan the QR code below or type the address in your browser's search bar.

https://pixelfy.me/hBgDtj

Thank you for your time and for supporting our work!

Best regards,
The Kroko Publishing Team

YOU ARE A WONDERFUL BOY
EMMA WRIGHT
Inspiring Stories about self-confidence, inner strength, and courage
KROKO VERLAG

CONTENTS

PROLOGUE

WHY ARE STORIES IMPORTANT AND VALUABLE?

Stories accompany us through everyday life. They are told to us, we read them, or we experience them ourselves. They show us new perspectives, and we learn from them.

Furthermore, they make us laugh and comfort us through support and hope. We do not feel alone when we find ourselves in stories with our longings, joys, and sorrows.

We are in the company of characters who share our feelings and thoughts and sometimes grow as close to our hearts as real people.

BECAUSE YOU ARE A MAGICAL BOY

The following stories are about worries, problems, and hardships.

Our main characters are boys with a particular characteristic that sets them apart from other boys and, therefore, encounter challenges all on their own.

In the process, they learn to find a solution to their problems through self-confidence, inner strength, and courage. Hugo, Max, Fridolin, Anton, Matt, and Basti manage in their stories to grow a bit more from their challenges.

The stories are about self-confidence, inner strength, and courage. Here lays the focus of this children's book because you can't necessarily separate the contents from each other.

Self-confidence always requires some inner strength, and inner strength often requires a fair amount of courage.

INSTEAD OF A TABLE OF CONTENTS. WE WILL BRIEFLY INTRODUCE OUR MAIN CHARACTERS:

Hugo, the pink chameleon, learns to adopt colors at school, but when he is insecure or upset, he constantly changes to his favorite color, pink. Hugo realizes he doesn't have to do everything right and is allowed to be different from the other chameleon boys. It is not a flaw; instead, he is unique with it and can still find recognition and affection.

Max has grown faster in recent months than his classmates, who call him Matchstick or Asparagus Max. Although he is becoming an outsider from the other boys, the friendliest girl in the class likes him.

She feels comfortable with him because Max listens and does not put himself in the center of everything when playing, which gives him the self-confidence he needs.

Fridolin is mourning the death of his grandpa, to whom he could always go when he had problems. Grandpa left him a box with lots of little things from their time together. There was also a bottle with a cork and a letter in it. The letter says that he lives on as a genie for him - his grandson.

When Fridolin misses him, all Fridolin has to do is open the bottle. He then feels the presence of his grandpa's love and hears his excellent advice in his mind. Through this, Fridolin learns that being sad is part of life and that he is strong enough to endure those sad feelings.

Anton undertakes an entirely unplanned crazy journey. On a small island, he runs into a group of giants. Although they are at least five times his size, he is not impressed by their size because of his inner strength.

With cleverness and gifts, he makes them his friends. They are unfortunate that he does not want to become their king when he has to leave.

Matt is afraid: even of mice. One day he falls asleep in the yard, and wild animals are chasing him in his dreams. He screams and suddenly wakes up because something soft is snuggling up at him.

The neighbor's little dog has come to comfort him. The little boy realizes that fear can't protect him, but he also doesn't need to be afraid for no reason.

Then his best friend Thea confesses to Basti that she is in love with him, and Basti becomes quite uncertain. He doesn't want her as a girlfriend, but he doesn't want to lose her as a best friend.

He is looking for advice from his mother. She says: Be honest with Thea; she deserves it. One day Basti gathers all his courage and tells her how he feels. Although a little sad, she understands their friendship's vital to him.

Of course, every child can read the stories - boy or girl, older or younger. However, they are primarily intended for boys who can already read by themself. Besides, no one should ever feel too old for children's stories.

SELF-CONFIDENCE: CHAPTER 1

HUGO. THE PINK CHAMELEON

Hugo yawns. He has just woken up after a good sleep in his tree with all the big green leaves. Heartily he yawns a second time.

Now it's his time to look around for a good breakfast.

Hugo looks down with one eye and watches with the other at all the leaves above him.

There must be a yummy bug somewhere?

He didn't finish his thoughts when right at this moment, a fat fly approached him from behind and buzzed carelessly around his motionless body.

Hugo quietly observes the insect closely with his big eyes. As it becomes cheekier and gets too close to his nose, his tongue lurches forward, and "flabbily," he has swallowed it.

That was delicious; he thought another big one of these growlers would make his day!

Suddenly he realizes that he doesn't have any time at all. Today is a fantastic and unforgettable day; by thinking about it, Hugo suddenly gets excited.

Today is his first day of school, and he will learn how a chameleon changes its color.

If he practices a lot, he will eventually be able to do it as quickly as the grown-up chameleons.

Hugo is not full yet. He's still craving a fat fly but knows from his mom that you can't study too well with a full stomach. Because the blood moves from the head to the stomach for digestion, his mom explained to him once.

She said, "that without blood in the head, the body gets tired."

When he thinks about it, he immediately closes one eye. With the other, he squints over at his parents, who were sleeping a few trees away.

They've probably just had breakfast, too, he was thinking.

He watched his dad as he slowly got ready to go on his way. Hugo saw him as he winked goodbye to his mom with both eyes simultaneously. Then he begins his descent.

Daddy is not in a hurry and bobs slowly back and forth, chameleon-style, with each step.

Back and forth, back and forth, he climbs leisurely towards the forest floor.

Hugo's dad has to do some work. His chores for today are to search for the giant larvae for dinner.

Meanwhile, Hugo's Mama licks the morning dew from the leaves, on which he can then lay the larvae when he returns this evening.

Hugo keeps one eye on his Mama, and she also squints over at him. Then she briefly unrolls her tail and curls it back up, a sign for Hugo that it is time to leave.

Thoughtfully, like his daddy, he slowly bobs back and forth down the tree trunk.

Of course, Hugo could also climb from branch to branch with his grasping tail. That way, he would get to school much faster, but suddenly he was not in such a hurry.

He is thinking and wondering about what the other chameleon children are like.

Will it be hard to learn to change color?

The closer Hugo gets to the school, the slower he bobs along.

“School for newly hatched chameleons,” as it is called in its entirety, is located in a small open grass area in the middle of the jungle.

Here, the young chameleons learn not to write and count like human children but everything necessary in a chameleon’s life.

The teacher, Mrs. Pinchpaw, is a big old chameleon lady who has just turned in a menacing yellow-green-black to make an impression on her new students.

She has clamped her toes on a drooping branch and is looking down on the unicolored, as she calls the little chameleons, from above.

A group of five chameleons of different sizes forms a semicircle on the leafy ground. Just a little apart, they squat on leaves and broken twigs to be a little more comfortable.

Hugo has been shimmering light blue and lime green since he hatched. A short distance from him sits the smallest chameleon of the group, a milk-white single-color girl named Beate.

She nervously bobs back and forth, earning a stern look from the teacher’s right eye.

Hugo likes little white Beate right away.

He doesn't notice that his skin has changed to a hint of pink as he looks at her.

The teacher, on the other hand, does not miss it. She directs both eyes sternly at the other single-color students.

She calls their attention firmly to the fact that Hugo already has some talent for changing colors.

Ashamed and delighted by the praise, Hugo looks up with one eye and back with the other to avoid looking at anyone.

At dinner with his parents, Hugo proudly talks about his first day at school. A delicious larva lies on a leaf in front of him, but Hugo is too tired to eat.

An exhausting day comes to an end for him.

It is already quite dark in the jungle, and the night creatures are waking up.

Tired to the point of falling over, Hugo moves over to his favorite branch.

Like his mom taught him, he wraps his tail tightly

around it before falling asleep.

Chameleons do that so they cannot fall off during the night.

Then Hugo makes himself comfortable and is asleep immediately, dreaming of glowing in all the rainbow colors when growing up.

He is no longer afraid of the coming school day but is excited.

Where is Beate? Mrs. Pinchpaw is turning red like blood, and as she straightens, she shows the scaly crest on her back.

She looks very dangerous.

Some students are bobbing back and forth with excitement, but Hugo isn't paying attention. His eyes roll in all directions.

He notices a small snake hurrying to wriggle past the chameleon group.

There were also two monkeys sitting in a tree. The teacher hisses threateningly in his direction.

Hugo lowers his head and makes himself even smaller than he already is.

But too late!

She tells him to hurry to the center of the group. She wants him to show the other chameleon children how to turn red.

But Hugo doesn't know how to do it; he hasn't listened to the teacher the day before.

He tries to think about the color red very hard, but nothing happens.

Does he wonder if he might have to hold his breath?

Nothing! Only his little nose horn turns red, and he has to sneeze from exertion.

Mrs. Pinchpaw repeats what a chameleon must do to turn red: It must imagine something threatening.

The other little chameleon snort and hiss, stand up, or bob at twice the average speed.

One gets an unusual red-colored head, and another a red leg, but only one; that looks funny.

Hugo can't manage to imagine anyone or anything he doesn't like or could be a threat to him.

So far, everyone has always been friendly to him.

Would the little snake from before be threatening?

He thinks about the snake and then looks back up to his tail.

Nothing has changed. It is still light blue-lime green and already a little bit pink again.

School is over for today again, and Mrs. Pinchpaw sends all the chameleon children home.

As a farewell, she adopts a nice dark green color.

On the way home, Hugo is not as proud of himself as he was the day before. He had hoped that turning red would be as easy as turning pink.

It is cold the following day in Hugo's forest, and he wishes he could breathe fire like his ancestors, the dragons.

His mother once told him a bedtime story about dragons. She said they lived long ago and were huge and very strong.

Hugo feels very small right now, and he is cold.

Only three chameleon children are squatting on the leafy forest floor this morning.

Mrs. Pinchpaw clings to her branch again and explains what a chameleon can do against the cold.

In one fell; swoop, she turns from green-blue to black.

Everyone wonders, why black?

There is a reason for this, she explains immediately. The skin can absorb the sun much better this way.

It is not difficult for the little dragons to follow her example this morning. And Hugo does succeed in getting at least half black.

Mrs. Pinchpaw gives him an acknowledging hiss for this.

A bright and shiny head peeks out from between the dense fallen leaves. Beate!

Hugo suddenly feels warm, and not only around the heart. He does not notice the external change that is taking place in his body.

Hugo only has eyes for the little milk-white chameleon girl.

He is only surprised that suddenly everyone is looking at him and no longer at Beate or the teacher.

Just a moment ago, Hugo was almost black.

Now, suddenly, the scales on his skin are shimmering in every shade of pink you can imagine.

Beate's scaly skin has also taken on a pinkish hue.

Mrs. Pinchpaw looks from Hugo to Beate and from Beate back to Hugo. Then she waggles her head thoughtfully.

Beate lowers her head but squints one eye at the teacher and the other at Hugo.

Mrs. Pinchpaw explains that Hugo's discoloration is very unusual. Usually, it is the females that take on such a light coloration.

At least everyone could see that Hugo was no longer cold. He had already anticipated the next lesson, she adds.

Chameleons lose their bright color in the blazing sun to protect themselves from it.

Although the teacher didn't mean her explanation incorrectly, Hugo is ashamed. He turns pink like a girl!

He no longer hears what else Mrs. Pinchpaw says, and he also no longer dares to look at Beate.

Not even with one eye.

A giant delicious maggot is sitting right in front of his nose on a small branch, but Hugo doesn't see it.

His eyes have turned inward, and the scales on his skin are pale.

He looks sick. Hugo's mom looks down at her son from a branch in the neighboring tree.

She worries; he even forgets to bob when a giant bird flies by.

Rocking like a leaf in the wind means camouflaging yourself from enemies.

His mom always practiced this with her children after they hatched.

With Hugo now, she is saddened to see her boy so sad.

She can't guess his sorrow. Hugo just sat on his tree in the morning. He curled his tail tightly around a branch and hasn't moved since.

Why doesn't Hugo want to go to school anymore?

What happened?

Hugo doesn't even eat the teeny-tiny larva that his dad brings over on a leaf. He was hunting for a whole day and the entire night.

Hugo's scaly skin gets paler and paler, even though it cools down during the night. Also saddened, Hugo's dad climbs down the tree trunk.

There is a rustling under Hugo's tree, and he looks down.

Led by the teacher Mrs. Pinchpaw four little chameleons are wiggling up the tree trunk in a seesaw walk.

Ignoring Hugo, the teacher climbs onto a higher branch and wraps her tail around it.

The other chameleon children spread out on all the tree branches around Hugo.

Beate is the last to reach the top.

Hugo slides to the side in his most beautiful pink to make room for her.

Beate's light scales have also acquired solid pink spots.

As if it were the most normal thing in the world to move with the school to the student, Mrs. Pinchpaw begins her lesson.

Today it's about the correct clamp grip on a branch. Hugo already knows the lesson from his mom. She has emphasized teaching her son, from hatching on how to hold on to even the narrowest twig.

Hugo is also far too excited to listen. Thoughts and feelings swirl around inside him, and you can barely miss it. Red spots appear on his head and the tip of his tail. For this, he immediately receives an appreciative bob from his class.

In a moment, Hugo feels a little better.

His class has come to see him, even though he always turns pink with embarrassment. He feels he doesn't do everything right in class on time.

Maybe it's just that Hugo needs a little longer, and it will work out in time.

Since he is feeling relaxed now, Hugo has returned to his normal light blue-green coloring.

The lesson passes quickly. The little chameleons, led by their teacher, slowly wiggle down Hugo's tree, one after the other, at a proper distance.

Only Beate dawdles around. She peers upward with one eye as if she has spotted an interesting bug in the treetop.

With the other eye, she squints at Hugo, who is already turning pink again from embarrassment.

Beate is thrilled. Hugo is the only chameleon boy who can look like her. To her, he is the most beautiful chameleon of all.

She tightly wraps her tail around his tail to show him what she feels.

With joy, Hugo turns as dark pink as never before. He is proud of himself! He understands that sometimes being unique to someone you like is enough.

Tailed together, the two little chameleons sit on Hugo's branch until the sun sets.

SELF-CONFIDENCE: CHAPTER 2

ASPARAGUS MAX

Max almost stumbles. Darn, so close to the goal! He has just stepped on the open lace of his new soccer boots.

When he bends down to tie it, a ball whistles right over his head; that was a close one, almost hit me, he thought.

“Thin asparagus! Matchstick! Lanky giant!” a couple of boys from his grade mock him.

They don’t want Max on their team.

It annoys Max a lot, even though it’s true.

In the last six months, he has grown faster than his classmates and towers over them by almost ten inches.

He thought; the others were still growing, just a little later.

But growth has also made him a bit clumsy.

Max feels the growth in his body. When he lies in his bed at night, his legs and sometimes even his feet hurt.

His mom reassured him that this was normal and would stop the day when he was fully grown.

lso, Aunt Klara told him that his father at Max's age was also a "bean pole," clumsy and awkward.

His arms and legs would always have been in the way. Or at least that's how it would have looked.

Max liked that word bean pole, though!

Playing soccer is not even really fun for him. Not only because the other boys don't want to play with him.

Julius, who always wants to be the best at everything, is the worst.

Mr. Lehwald, the sports teacher, has noticed this. But he says he doesn't want to interfere; they should work it out among themselves. They should learn to talk to each other and solve their problems without an adult constantly interfering.

Max also thinks that the teacher is right and children need to be able to work things out among themselves.

However, his mom feels the teacher is taking it too easy. If his classmates continue to annoy

Max, she wants to talk to Mr. Lehwald.

Max would instead find another solution.

Saskia, who everyone calls Sassi, is the most popular girl in the class. She is also slightly taller than all her female classmates, but the girls don't mind.

Sassi is not only pretty but also lovely to everyone, something Max already noticed on the first day of school - and not just him.

Julius always sneaks around her during their breaks and often repeats what she has said in class.

Sassi pretends not to notice and doesn't respond to him. She prefers to talk to the other girls in her class.

The school bell calls for class, and everyone runs off simultaneously.

No one notices when Max gets pushed from behind.

As he stumbles, his glasses fly off his nose and end up right in front of Sassi's feet.

Julius yells, “It’s your fault, Asparagus Max!” when he runs past them.

As he does, he looks at Sassi questioningly to see if he has made an impression on her.

“Watch out, don’t step on it!” Sassi holds a girl at a distance with one hand as she bends down to pick up Max’s glasses.

He’s stood up by now, and his pants have a tear across his knee. It is also bleeding slightly.

“Thanks!” says Max, taking the glasses from Sassi, who holds them out to him.

“That doesn’t look good.

You should go to see the school nurse and get it checked out.

You might need a Band-Aid put on it.”

“Nah, it’s okay; I’m already late for my class anyway” Max replied.

Max tries not to show that his bleeding knee does hurt him a little. He’s happy to see how worried Saskia is about him.

At home, his mom first sewed the tear and put a patch over it. Max has chosen a patch with a fox.

The following day, he saw Sassi pushing her bike in front of the school gate.

She has a flat tire.

Max said right away, “I can patch that for you! This afternoon if you want?

My uncle showed me how to do that”, he said.

“You just take out the inner tube and look underwater for air bubbles. Follow the bubbles and that’s the place where you have to patch it”.

“It is easy to patch it over.” Max added.

“Just like your pants,” Sassi laughs.

“Really cool, the fox. Is that a sly fox like you?”

Later that day, Max removes the inner tube and looks for the leak while Sassi watches him.

Max didn’t tell her he had called his uncle beforehand and questioned him for every step to fix Sassi’s bicycle tire.

He doesn't want to do anything wrong and wants to impress Sassi.

Max also brought a repair instruction and read it carefully while following it step by step. While reading, he pushes his glasses up a bit on his nose from time to time.

It puts a smile on Sassi's face.

"I like that!" she said.

"What?" Max is asking.

"You're different from the other boys in our class. What you do, you want to do right. The boys I know always just want everyone to think they're great. For what? For nothing?"

Max says nothing. He doesn't want to disappoint Sassi. He, too, wants her to think he's excellent.

After he fixed the tire, Max and Sassi sat next to each other on the grass.

Sassi picks all the daisies she can reach while sitting down.

She makes a wreath out of them, putting it on her hair after she finishes.

Max watches her. He thinks about what she said earlier about being different.

"Do you know I was the smallest in kindergarten?" she said.

"Even the teachers called me 'dwarf.' I didn't grow until I got to school," Sassi said.

"And how did you feel?" asks Max.

"Dumb! Like I didn't belong there. Even though the teachers meant it nicely."

Max nods and answers. "Yes, being different is often a silly feeling!"

"But why does everyone have to be the same, anyway? That's boring as hell!"

All of a sudden, Sassi jumps up and runs to her bike.

"I have to go home; she says while hurrying to her bike.

"I'll see you at school tomorrow. Thanks, Max."

Max gets up, too. He watches her until she disappears around the corner. Then he goes into the house.

In small groups, all the children meet in the yard before entering the school.

When the school bell rings, they run together to their classrooms. Sassi is sitting on a bench.

When she sees Max entering the courtyard, she takes off her right shoe. Sassi waves him over with her shoe and tells him to sit beside her.

“Quick, take off your right shoe, we’ll swap a sock! I want to try something!”

Max gives Sassi a stunning look but follows her request. He holds out a blue sock for her and accepts her red one.

A few stragglers run to the school door when the bell rings. Max slips into his shoes and ties them while Sassi, who has shoes to fall into, is already running ahead.

“It’s best if we don’t arrive in class together. Then everyone won’t notice right away. See you later!”

Max pulls the legs of his pants down. He doesn’t want everyone to see his socks right away while he is the last to arrive in class. He hasn’t noticed his teacher walking behind him and almost bangs the classroom door on his head.

“Oh! I didn’t see you. Sorry, Mr. Werner,” Max mumbles sheepishly, and Julius and his friends are already grinning again in the back row.

“Asparagus Max! Clumsy again!”

They whisper just loud enough for Max to hear. Sassi looks at the homework sheet that Mr. Werner has just handed out. She is sitting on the other side of the classroom.

Did she hear it?

Max slides back and forth restlessly in his chair. He is not listening to what the teacher is telling them.

“Max, what’s going on? Do you need to step out?”

Max shakes his head. He at least tries to listen for the rest of the lesson. Even though he keeps thinking about Sassi’s plan.

Luca, Julius’ friend, first notices Max wearing two different socks.

“Look, the looser, the beanpole - wears two different socks.

Are you also color blind - you’ve got glasses, too.”

Max says nothing.

Now Sassi makes her entrance. She proudly shows the other girls her red and her blue socks. Some girls shake their heads.

“That’s fashion now,” she said. All over Europe, they already wear this in school. I saw it on social media,” Sassi claims.

Immediately, the mood changes. Everyone wants to know where.

“I don’t remember exactly,” she deflects.

“Look, Max has seen the video too!” shouted Svenja, sitting next to Sassi.

“Yes, blue and red is really in! Just like yellow and green or pink and purple!”

“Really cool, Sassi!” Julius says quickly.

Max turns away and trying not to laugh.

After school, Max dawdles around until it’s quiet in the hallway. Sassi is in no hurry, either. She asks Mr. Werner for something for her homework. Max is waiting patiently for her.

“Come on, Sassi, lets swap socks again. My mom would be surprised ...”

Sassi holds out his blue sock to Max, putting it back on.

“Sassi, you lied to the others. There’s no video at all.” Max grins.

“It’s no big deal. If it would have hurt someone, I wouldn’t have done it.”

Sassi unlocks her bike and pushes it alongside Max.

“And besides, there’s all kinds of stuff on the Internet. Any bets that tomorrow at least Julius and Luca will be wearing different socks?”

“Yeah, and maybe a few more girls. So, what’s your plan, Sassi?”

“Nothing special, just wait and see.”

Max got curious, but he trusted Sassi.

“Want to do homework together later?” she asks.

Max nods enthusiastically with a big grin all over his face.

Sassi walks with him to the next street corner. Then she gets on her bike and waves goodbye to him.

At home, Max's mom is already waiting for him with dinner.

Max is very hungry. "I can't get you full today," she jokes.

"Yeah, I think I want to change and want to get bigger!" Or better, just more robust!"

"But strength isn't just about power," Max's mom replies.

"Will you help me clear the table before you do your homework?"

Max replies: "Sassi from my classmate will be here soon. We want to study together."

"That's a good idea." His mom says and is walking smiling into the kitchen.

The following day Max is looking forward to going to school for the first time. He's going to see Sassi.

She told him a secret yesterday afternoon during their homework. A secret that not even Svenja knows, and Max is mighty proud of that.

She doesn't seem to care if he's skinny and tall and wears glasses.

When he walks into the classroom, everyone looks at his feet. Some faces disapprovingly wrinkle because Max wears two identical green socks.

He pretends not to notice them and sits down on his desk.

Sassi was right. Half the class believed her joke and wore different socks on their feet.

Sassi appears last in class today wearing pink and blue striped socks, and everyone looks at her feet.

"But identical socks aren't cool, are they?" asks Julius, a little uncertainly.

"Well, I think my socks are nice, so I wear them on both feet." Sassi replied.

"I don't get it, yesterday you wear ..." Julius stopped, confused.

"Do you like it, or do you only do it because the others do it?"

“I don’t have to like everything others think is great.” She says and sits down in her seat and unpacks her school supplies.

“You made that up yesterday, didn’t you?” whispers Svenja.

Sassi shrugs her shoulders in response with a smile.

Max isn’t listening to Mr. Werner today, either. He thinks he has learned much more from Sassi today than he can learn in school, and that feels good.

Max eats an apple during the break and watches the girls standing around Sassi. They are laughing out loud about something.

A few days ago, he would have thought they were laughing at him. Today he thinks it’s okay not to like soccer, to be a little clumsy, and to have grown too fast. He can still make friends.

“Doing everything Sassi tells you to do now, I guess?” he heard Julius saying behind him. He’s brought Luca along for backup.

Sassi sees this and comes over to them, but she doesn’t have to defend Max.

He self-confidently replied to Julius. “No, I’ll do what I like! I don’t want to be like everyone else. Not anymore! In a few years, maybe I won’t be the only tall and skinny one. But that’s the way it is for now.”

Max turns around and leaves Julius standing, surprised there.

Sassi gives him a thumbs up; everyone can see how proud she is of Max.

INNER STRENGTH: CHAPTER 1

THE GENIE IN THE BOTTLE

“Frido! Frido!” Grandpa Franz calls after him.

Fridolin shakes his head sadly. His grandpa’s voice is not coming from him but his memory. Everything in this old house reminds him of his Grandpa Franz.

Ever since Fridolin can remember, he has visited him here. Later, when Grandpa needed help, Frido and the whole family moved in with him.

That was great! How much fun was it to prank each other?

How often he played hide-and-seek with Grandpa in the old house. There couldn’t have been a more beautiful place than this house with all its corners for this game.

Grandpa often pretended not to see him, even when standing right in front of Frido’s hiding place.

In exchange, he let his grandpa win at “Homeward Bound,” Not always, but sometimes. I wonder if grandpa knew that.

When he wants to be left alone, Frido sits down

on the top of the stairs to the attic.

It's very dusty up there. Because no one ever climbs up here, therefore it's not cleaned very often.

That's why Frido is sitting on these stairs now. He has retreated here because he doesn't want to talk to anyone. Not with Grandma, Mom, and Uncle Claus or all the other people sitting at the table downstairs in the big dining room.

They're drinking coffee and eating cake.

When the door to the stairwell opens, Frido can hear the dishes clattering and the forks clinking beside all the voices.

But he can't understand what they're saying, nor does he want to.

He wants to think about Grandpa.

Today they all said goodbye to him at the cemetery.

Frido didn't want to go there and didn't have to; with Aunt Klara, he had set the coffee table where everyone was sitting.

There is a squeaking noise behind Fridolin.

Maunzer, the cat, has pushed the door to the attic open, which was only ajar.

The attic is one big room with a few slanted skylight windows. A light bulb hangs from the ceiling in the middle of the room.

Everything the family can no longer use is stored away up there. Old cupboards and chests with drawers, broken armchairs and lots of boxes with clothes and books, broken dishes, and dented pots. Toys, picture frames, an old crib, and mattresses with springs sticking out.

The attic is Maunzer's kingdom! He always catches mice and puts them on Grandma Anna's doormat at the entrance.

Grandpa Franz always laughed about it and said it was her present. She always had to thank Maunzer properly for it.

Grandpa whispered to him that the mice Maunzer dragged in probably all died of old age. The cat simply collects the mice on his rounds and brings them to Grandma Anna.

Fridolin has to grin when he thinks about it.

Maunzer sits down with him and presses his

head into Frido's hand. That means; pet me.

Frido fulfills his wish and gently scratches the old cat behind the ears. Maunzer also seems to notice that something is wrong.

The guests leave one after the other. Frido can only understand snatches of sentences or single comforting words. Anyway, he doesn't want to hear them.

So, he closes his eyes and presses his hands firmly over his ears. When he takes them down again, everything is as before. The visitors will all be gone.

No, they didn't sit at the table today; it's a day like any other, and soon Grandpa will come up the stairs. Slowly as always, with one hand on the railing, thinking about a new game he could play with him.

Fridolin believes quite firmly that it was all just a bad dream that had happened the last few days.

Fridolin counts to ten. And then, just to be on the safe side, he counts again. He drops his hands and opens his eyes, blinking.

No grandpa is on the stairs, and neither does he hear his footsteps climbing up. Only the front door slams shut at the bottom of the stairs.

“Have you seen Frido?” asks Mama Aunt Klara, who is just crossing the hallway into the kitchen with a tray full of dishes.

“No. Not since we set the table. Maybe he’s outside or in the garden.”

His mom yanks open the front door and call for him quite loudly. He hears it only very softly on the stairs, almost not at all. That’s why he can pretend he didn’t listen to her.

“Let him be. I think he’d rather be alone,” Aunt Klara says sympathetically.

Feelings you don’t understand can be pretty exhausting, Fridolin realizes. His eyes fall shut from tiredness.

Snuggled up close to Maunzer, he falls asleep on the stairs.

He wakes up when he feels a gentle touch on his cheek. His mom leans over him and holds out her hand.

"You can come down, sweetheart. Everybody's gone. Only Aunt Klara, Grandma Anna and Papa are still here."

Fridolin sleepily straightens up.

Maunzer lives up to his name. He grunts when Frido pulls away his arm, which has served as a pillow for the cat.

"Are you hungry?" his mom implores him.

Frido shakes his head.

"Then come with me, Papa has something Grandpa Franz gave him for you."

Frido holds his mommy's hand tightly and walks downstairs with her.

Fridolin's dad takes his son very tightly in his arms.

They stand in the middle of the room for a while without speaking a word, both crying softly.

Then Papa blows his nose into a big handkerchief while he sits in Grandpa's recliner. He pulls Fridolin gently onto his lap.

“Being sad is perfectly normal. If you want to cry, then cry”, Dad says.

“Grandpa Franz was my dad after all. Like you, I’ve known him since I came into the world. I will miss him terribly. We will all miss him, you perhaps most of all”.

Do you know that sometimes I envied you a little?”

Fridolin looks at his father questioningly. He shakes his head.

“When I was your age, like you are now, Grandpa Franz had to work. When he came home in the evening, he was tired and didn’t always feel like playing with me”.

“For you, he always had time. You could do all the great things with him that he couldn’t do with me. And you were so much alike. That made me happy.”

Fridolin’s dad wipes a tear from one eye. He puts Fridolin on the floor, gets up, and walks out of the room.

In the hallway, a closet door creaks.

The next moment, his dad is standing in the

doorway again. He holds a wooden box in his hands.

“Grandpa Franz gave this to me for you.”

Fridolin’s eyes widen. What’s in the box, and why didn’t his grandpa give it to him himself, he wonders. His dad seems to be able to read his mind.

“You know that Grandpa Franz was quite old, and in the last few weeks he was also very sick.”

Fridolin remembers that lately, his grandpa often had to take breaks from playing and walking because he didn’t breathe well when they played too much.

“And what’s in the box?” asks Fridolin.

“I don’t know that either; it’s just for you. Go and see for yourself. It’s best if you take it into your room and look inside when you’re alone,” dad answers and hands Fridolin his box.

After looking at the box from all sides, Fridolin is ready to look inside.

He takes the box on his lap and carefully opens the lid. His heart pounds faster; he has received a real treasure chest.

Grandpa has stored all kinds of little things in it.

It reminds him of their trips, games, and adventures together.

Tickets, postcards, a photo album, toys he thought were lost, even his pacifier and Grandpa's old glasses, from which the lenses had fallen out.

When Fridolin read, he always put them on his nose and imitated Grandpa reading aloud.

But what Fridolin finds most interesting is an empty bottle. It has a thick belly and a cork. Around the neck of the bottle hangs a letter that says 'FRIDOLIN' in big letters.

Frido's heart is pounding now even more with excitement as he tears open the letter. He skims over the spidery printed letters, then slowly rereads everything from the beginning. It says:

"My dear Frido!

You must believe one thing: I would have liked to keep you company for a little longer. But it was not meant to be. My body is old and sick. It shows me that it wants to rest forever. That an older person has no more strength is normal and *is part of life. Even if I don't want that, I know you are sad now. That is also part of life. And I know you are strong enough not to run away from sadness but to endure it. You are not alone. Around you are mom and dad, grandma Anna, aunt Klara and all the others who love you very much."*

"Think of it this way: only my old, sick body has left you. But we have experienced so many beautiful things together, which you will be able to remember all your life. So, I will stay with you in your memory and in your heart. I have turned into a Genie to make it easier for you, as long as you are little."

Frido has to swallow, but he feels a lump in his throat. He wipes the tears from his cheeks with the sleeve of his sweater and continues reading.

But before he does, he puts his grandfather's old glasses on his nose. He should have done that sooner so that he could hear Grandpa's voice in his mind reading the letter to him.

"It is best to put the bottle next to your bed. Sadness often comes in the evening when you are no longer busy with homework, games, or anything else. When you feel alone, open the

bottle. I will come out, and you can tell me all your worries and troubles, just like you always did. You can't see me, but I will be there to listen to you."

The lump is there again, and Frido has to swallow several times. He digs in the box and fishes out the photo album.

Without Fridolin noticing, Maunzer sneaks into the room and lies down next to him. Fridolin opens the album, flips through it, and gets stuck on a picture.

"Look, Maunzer, that's when Grandpa and I went to the zoo. You see, there's a tiger in the back. He looks a little like you - only much bigger."

The cat purrs but otherwise shows little interest in his larger kin.

A smile flitted across Frido's face and landed on the picture. He puffs out his cheeks and blows out all the air causing it to fly off. Then he continues reading the letter:

"There is so much I would still like to tell you. However, I would have to write a book to fit it all on paper. That's why I'll only tell you the most important things: You are as funny as your

name. That's probably why you often play tricks on me. How glad I was you played them on me. But you also asked me serious questions, and I always had to think carefully before answering. You walk through life with your eyes open. You put bugs on the grass so that no one steps on them and paint the house wall colourful so that everything doesn't look so gray in winter. All this and much more shows me what a wonderful, sensitive, smart, funny, and strong boy you are. If you ever lose heart, remember that! Bad days are the opposite of good days, and many more good days will come." "I love you very much!"

"Your Grandpa"

Fridolin lowers the paper. He puts the bottle on the nightstand and snuggles under his blanket with Maunzer.

When the letter fell to the floor, he discovered his grandpa had written something else on the back.

"P.S. Please always cork the bottle after you have talked to me. After all, I need some rest, too!"

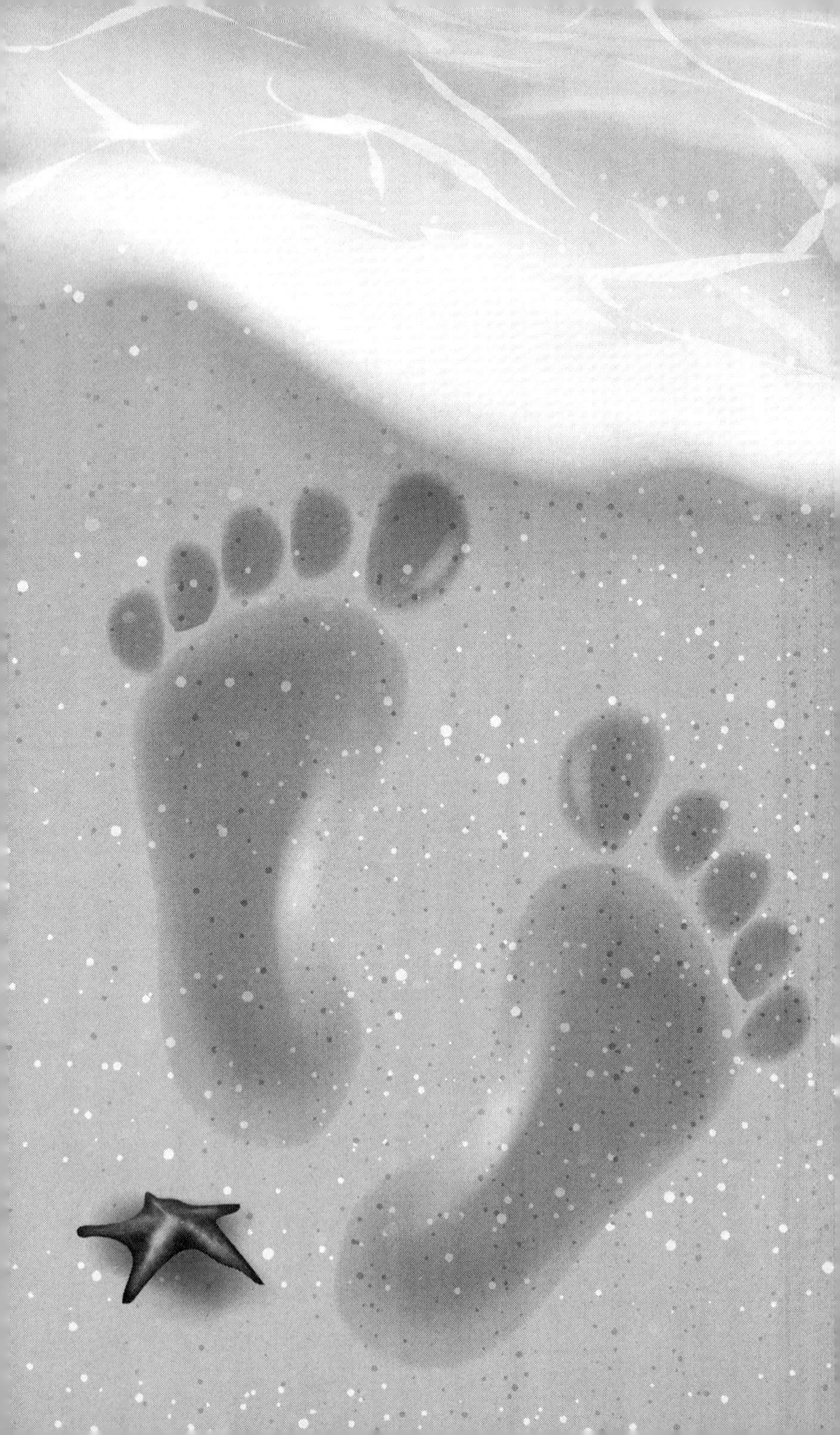

INNER STRENGTH: CHAPTER 2

THE ISLAND OF THE BIG GUYS

There is nothing better for Anton than being on the water in his rubber dinghy.

He loves to lie in it on his back and look at the sky.

He loves hanging his feet in the water and waiting for a fish to nibble on his toes. Or even just daydreaming away at the sight of the sparkling water.

Sometimes he paddles a bit, then drifts again on the small lake, where he quickly reaches the other shore.

A cloud has pushed in front of the sun, and the wind is coming up. A gust sweeps across the small lake, and the water begins to ripple in small waves.

As if pulled by magic, the small inflatable boat starts to move. It drifts faster and faster toward the opposite shore.

Anton doesn't want to go there at all.

He reaches for his paddle to steer against it. He can't fight the current; his strength is not enough, and his dinghy should hit the shore any moment.

Anton checks that his life jacket is tight and braces himself for a jolt. He can already reach the first stalks of grass on the shore and can hold on.

The grassland in front of him splits.

The gap reveals a little stream into which the lake's water presses with a gurgling sound.

Pointed rocks rise from the water in some places. Just one crack and the air escapes from the tube of the rubber boat.

To prevent this, Anton tries to keep his distance from the rocks with the paddle. In doing so, he has to be careful not to fall out of the boat himself.

It is so exhausting that he doesn't even get to worry about where the journey will take him.

The little boat bounces on the small waves but miraculously doesn't get stuck anywhere.

The current pulls it further and further along. At some point, Anton gives up trying to paddle against it.

When the current calm down, the stream has

already doubled in width and has become a river.

The river has become very wide when the sun sinks into the horizon a few hours later. The banks are barely visible from the middle, where Anton is still drifting.

He is now sure that his dinghy is drifting out to sea. Admittedly, this is a confounding situation.

Of course, Anton is scared of being alone in the dark but has no intention of giving up.

What else can he do but embark on an adventure? That's why he talks himself into believing that he can do it. Anton also tries not to cry because crying doesn't help him much in this situation.

Anton looks at his inflatable boat. It seems to him as if it has grown during the journey. He does a test: carefully stretches out his legs and doesn't bump his toes at the other end. His inflatable boat suddenly seems more stable, too.

At least it has brought him safely through the currents between the sharp rocks. That's a good sign. Maybe it will grow even more in the sea. Then it will speed up, and he will soon hit

Land again. This thought makes Anton feel more confident.

The sun has sunk into the sea. Fortunately, the clouds have dispersed. The sky is now so clear that Anton can see the moon and the stars.

He gazes at the sky in amazement, searching for familiar constellations. Tired from staring, his eyes fall closed, and Anton is fast asleep within seconds.

He dreams of sailing around the world on an old pirate ship and discovering new islands. At the top, from the lookout on the main mast, Anton can see the horizon. If he finds Land, he waves his free arm and calls out loudly, "Land ho!

Thick drops wake Anton. Rain? Anton licks his lips. It tastes salty. Seawater must have splashed into the boat.

Anton squints against the sun, which is already relatively high in the sky. Astonished, he looks around. The inflatable boat from last night has turned into a small sailboat with a tiny cabin in the middle.

The wind is blowing strongly into the single sail. The ship has picked up speed well.

Anton looks around in amazement. The boat has a real rudder for steering and is holding course for an as yet uncertain destination. Above him, a few seagulls accompany the sailboat.

Curious, Anton jiggles the door to the cabin. It sticks a little. The place has an actual bunk and a small galley. Anton has only recently read that this is the name given to the bed and kitchen on a ship.

Because he's now starving, Anton looks in the cupboards for something to eat. He finds a canister of drinking water, a ship's rusks, apples, and some nuts.

Rusks and apples have never tasted so good to him!

When he has had enough, Anton examines the rest of the cabin and discovers a package with the inscription 'ANTON' and 'DO NOT OPEN UNTIL YOUR BIRTHDAY.' That's right, Anton's birthday is tomorrow! Where does that come from, he wonders. And in the next moment thinks what a pity it is that he will probably have to celebrate it all by himself.

The following day, the boat suddenly begins to

rock. Still sleepy, Anton runs out of the cabin to look for the cause.

A couple of high-spirited dolphins are playing tag around the sailboat. They keep nudging it with their snouts to invite it to play with them.

He wonders if they will let him pet them. Anton holds his hand in the water, and a courageous little dolphin swim close to him. His skin feels very smooth and cool. One last nudge and the dolphins swim away.

Anton watches them go until he can no longer see them. Although they have disappeared, the sailboat is now no longer holding course.

Anton sits down at the helm and looks into the water. The color of the sea has changed. The dark blue is getting lighter and lighter.

He looks in all directions, and in the distance, he recognizes a green spot. He heads for it.

Soon he recognizes an island with tall palm trees towering along a white sandy beach. Between the palm trees are individual rocks.

Anton searches, mesmerized but discovers neither a human nor an animal there.

Slowly, the sailboat glides toward the beach until it gets stuck in the sand with a gentle jolt.

He hops off the boat into the water, which only reaches up to his bottom.

Something tickles his pants as he walks through crystal-clear water to the beach. A small, colorful fish slips out of his trouser leg and takes off.

Land under his feet again!

Walking barefoot through the warm sand feels excellent. Anton is amazed at the large shells he sees.

But what is this? A giant footprint?

Anton compares it to his footprint and measures the length of his foot five times.

While doing this, a shadow moves in front of the sun. Before he knew it, a giant hand grabbed him and lifted him.

At first, he can't make out a thing in the face he's looking at because of all the hair on his head. The colossal head approaches him, and Anton backs away from the big hand as far as he can.

But it is not the overgrown mouth that he suspects equally large teeth that approach him, but a gigantic nose.

The big guy sniffs at Anton. First very cautiously and then immediately a little more directly. Anton feels as if he wants to inhale him.

His heart drops into his pants. What should he do?

He can kick the giant in the nose or try to bite him. But even as he thinks about it, he realizes how futile the attempt would be.

He can't do anything here with physical strength. He must show the giant that he is strong in another way. How can he prove to him that he is not afraid of him? Anton pulls up both arms threateningly and shouts as loud as he can.

Startled, the giant almost drops him. Anton looks as angry as he can and points to the ground. The giant now looks more perplexed than dangerous.

Anton repeats his gesture, only this time a little more energetically. The giant raises his eyebrows to sign that he has understood and carefully sets Anton down on the sand. Anton's head is now not even level with the giant's knee.

More giants approach from the palm forest. Anton is getting nervous. But even they must not notice Anton's excitement. They should think that he is smaller but powerful. Therefore, he has no choice but to impress them.

But how? And with what? He remembers the package on his boat. In all the excitement, he has completely forgotten his birthday. Maybe there is something in the box that he can share with the giants.

To get his attention, Anton kicks the giant who picked him up very hard on the big toe. Then he points to his boat and uses sign language to clarify that he wants to get something and will be right back.

Anton stretches himself to appear as tall as possible. With his head proudly raised, he slowly steps aboard.

The giants gather around him curiously as Anton opens his package with great fanfare as if it alone were a magic trick.

The first thing he pulls out is a candle. He shows it around before placing it in the sand: followed by matches, sparklers, cardboard hats with rubber bands, and a large chocolate cake.

Anton hands each giant a sparkler and a cardboard hat and then lights the candle.

With a lit sparkler, he draws figures in the air. Grumbling and grunting, the giants express their applause. They seem impressed.

The first giant dares to light his sparkler and almost stumbles backward in fright when the sparks in his hand start to fly.

He has put his much too-small hat over his nose to protect himself. Now everyone lights their sparklers. The giants marvel enthusiastically at the small fireworks display. Each wears his little hat in a different place. One has hung it around his ear, and another has placed it on his big toe. Only Anton wears it on his head.

Finally, with a heavy heart, Anton divides up his special chocolate cake. He puts a small piece in his mouth and offers the rest of the cake to the giants.

Somewhat wistfully, Anton watches how quickly the cake disappears into the mouths of his new friends. A whole piece is no more to them than a small bite is to Anton.

They smack on the small piece for a long time. Anton is now no longer afraid of them. His birthday party was a complete success!

Night falls. All at once, the giants become pretty restless. They lash out and run wildly through the area.

Anton immediately gets to feel the reason himself. At dusk, mosquitoes descend on the island, and they buzz and buzz around them.

Anton collects dry palm leaves and makes a sign to the giants to help him.

When one of the giants pulls out an entire palm tree, he shakes his head vigorously. Only the dried palm leaves!

With his matches, he lights a campfire, which soon begins to smoke and drives away the mosquitoes.

The giants are thrilled! They take turns lifting Anton on their shoulders to cheer him on. In their growling and grunting language, they whisper, draw a crown in the sand, and point at Anton.

They talk to him with their hands and feet, which looks very funny.

It takes Anton a while until he understands what they want to tell him: You are much stronger than us and can even drive away the dangerous mosquitoes. Stay here and become our king.

Anton thanks them and also draws something in the sand. Then he points to the sea.

“There are a few people, so I must go back home. My family is waiting for me,” he says.

With heavy hearts, the giants let Anton go. As a farewell, they blow into his sail so that the sailboat picks up speed.

When Anton is back home in his bed, he is happy. He has had a great adventure! But he keeps that to himself because no one would believe his story about him, the strong guy.

COURAGE: CHAPTER 1

NO FEAR OF WILD ANIMALS

Matt is not entirely comfortable with his mother's suggestion that he do his chores outside in the garden. The weather is not nice today.

He would prefer to stay in his room, but the two workers are busy today.

They are repainting the ceiling in his room.

"So that it doesn't fall on your head," Dad joked. He didn't mean anything by it, but he hit the bull's eye.

Because Matt worries about everything, he often gets scared of things he doesn't know, especially animals.

They can run into him, knock him down and bite him or do something even worse to him. Crawling animals are terrifying to him. It didn't use to be so bad, but he gets creeped out more and more.

For his homework, Matt has to read a story. He takes the book into the garden in a huge basket. In addition to his book, Matt takes a pad, two blankets, and some pillows. Then he carries them outside to the lawn.

Matt unfolds the pad and straightens it at the corners. Then he puts the first one and another blanket on it, and finally, he sits in the middle and builds the cushions around himself like a wall.

Now Matt feels a little more comfortable and not so exposed. He would never sit down in a meadow without a pad just because of the bugs and spiders.

He starts to read. But he can't concentrate on the story. His thoughts jump from the handypersons in his room to Dad.

Dad wants to get his car from the garage. Then he thinks about Mom, who promised to bake cupcakes with him this weekend.

His tongue runs along his teeth, and he wonders if he needs braces. Matt tries hard to reread his story from the beginning. He has read the first paragraph three times now without being able to remember what it says. After a few words, his mind is somewhere else.

Last week he saw a mouse in the school bathroom and ran away screaming. Like a little girl! The boys in his class teased him about it all day.

When Matt thinks about it, he still feels embarrassed. Hopefully, his classmates will forget about it quickly.

Matt starts yawning. Overthinking makes him quite sleepy. On his fourth attempt to read the story for school, his eyes fall shut, and he immediately falls asleep.

The grass grows so fast that Matt can watch it. Within minutes, the stakes are a meter high and growing and growing. As they do, they grow firmer and firmer.

They push Matts's blankets together so much that he has to get up quickly. When he tries to stuff everything into his basket, the pillows get stuck between the stalks. He has to pull hard and tear a pillowcase in the process.

When he turns around to the house, Matt hears his mom stirring in a bowl through the open window and the workers shouting something.

He is surprised that no one in the house sees that the lawn has become a jungle.

Branches grow on all sides, and solid roots form on the ground. The canopy of leaves now reaches over Matt's head so that the sunlight barely goes through.

Panic-stricken, Matt calls for help. His mom must be able to hear him.

Pressing the basket protectively in front of his chest, Matt fights his way toward the house.

"This jungle must end somewhere," he thinks. He must have walked ten times further than the distance to the house by now. At least, that's how it seems to him.

Maybe the entire property has grown, too, it occurs to him. Then he gets the frightening idea of what has happened: It's not the grass that has grown, but he that has shrunk! He can no longer be more significant than a mouse.

A beetle as enormous as a full-grown German shepherd crawled right toward him. Matt is almost breathless with fright. His antennae move back and forth as he crawls, and his carapace glitters a beautiful golden green. Matt does not dare to move. He already thinks he feels the bite of the beetle on his thigh. But the beetle crawls, completely uninterested, right past him.

Matt follows him a little, hoping he can lead him to the house. Wherever he looks, in all directions, he sees stakes of grass that have become trees, reaching far above his head.

Not only is everything more significant, but the sounds have also become louder. When Matt can no longer see the beetle, Matt hears it running. Its abdominal carapace scrapes over the tiny bumps in the ground. When the stalks bend, it sounds like a tree falling over to Matt.

A loud noise erupts behind him. He turns around and sees a mouse as big as he is running towards him at high speed.

Matt is sure it will eat him. He holds his hands protectively in front of his face.

When nothing happens, he peeks between his fingers. The mouse has stopped in front of him. It looks at him in amazement from its plate-round black eyes. Then it runs past him, squeaking.

Astonished, Matt realizes that he has understood the squeak. It means, "Get out of here; the neighbour's cat is after me."

The next moment, Matt also hears a breathtaking snarl. He sees only a gigantic big paw right next to him. From above, a large black cat snout comes closer and closer to him.

Its mouth opens with pointed teeth as big as Matts's arm. It is too late to run away. He doesn't want to be eaten. He screams as loud as he can and never before in his life ...

Completely exhausted, Matt wakes up from his nightmare. Did he scream? His feelings still daze. Slowly he realizes that he only had a bad dream.

"I was lucky once again, he thinks." But he doesn't want to stay outside anymore. He tucks the blankets and pillows under his arm and walks into the house.

At the entrance, he turns around one more time. He feels he is being watched but can't spot anyone.

The house smells of cake up to Matt's room. To surprise him, his mother has already baked the promised muffins today.

Matt throws his things on the floor and storms into the kitchen.

His mom is just taking the little cakes out of the oven. Matt can hardly wait until the muffins have cooled down enough for him to take a bite.

He wonders if it will go faster if he opens all the windows and creates a breeze.

“It couldn’t hurt,” says Matt’s mother and takes the opportunity to ask him about his nightmare. She heard him screaming outside and knew he had had another bad dream.

As far as he can remember, he always tells her about his dreams. As he talks to her, he immediately gets another thick lump in his throat.

His mom listens attentively. Matt and her sometimes tell each other their dreams, especially the beautiful ones or the confusing ones.

Matt knows that the animals he was so afraid of in the dream are much smaller than him in real life and run away from him instead of biting him.

Because he has no reason to be like that, he wants to eliminate his fear, but he doesn’t know how. As soon as an animal gets too close, Matt fears it will bite him.

Mom says it wasn’t like that when he was little.

And that she hopes they can overcome the fear together. Matt can always talk to his mom. She doesn't make fun of him but listens to him and takes him seriously. And she bakes super yummy cupcakes! After that, everything is not so wrong anymore, and he feels relieved.

When Matt thinks about it, Mom is right. He is much bigger than a mouse. Even the mouse in the school bathroom ran away really fast. It was afraid of him and didn't want to bite him.

He decides to return to the garden the next sunny day and do his homework there. And when he sees an animal, he wants to wait and see how it feels to have it nearby. For him, this is a brave step. He can always run into the house if he gets scared.

The next day is beautiful garden weather. Matt gets his blankets and pillows. He doesn't want to do without yet and takes all his homework. With all this, he makes himself comfortable on the lawn like the day before.

A bird sits on the garden fence. It watches Matt for a while, then flies up a tree. Birds scare him less. They always fly off right away. Matt lies down on his stomach on the blanket and looks closely at the grass.

A few ants take the shortcut across the tip of his blanket. Like on the rails of his toy train, they run one after the other along a particular path. Matt is not interested in them. Seen from a little distance, they look pretty harmless and very tiny.

A few meters away, a giant beetle tries to climb up an old tree trunk.

After Matt slips and stands up again, he moves a little closer. The pincers on the front of its head already look dangerous.

He looks for a stick and gives the beetle a push. Suddenly, the bug is in a hurry to get past the tree, and Matt returns to his book. He carefully shakes off the ants from the cover and makes himself comfortable.

Today, his reading has improved, and he finished his tasks quickly. He feels too comfortable in the warm sun to go inside yet.

He stretches out on the blanket and closes his eyes. The neighbor's cat comes to his mind.

Mom said the cat usually doesn't go outside

until it gets dark. During the day, he sleeps. To be on the safe side, Matt lifts his head to see if he sees it running around somewhere. The air is clear. Far and wide, no tomcat. Matt closes his eyes again.

His old favorite teddy bear lies next to him, and he snuggles into him as he used to when he wanted some comfort.

He is so warm and soft. Matt feels safe and secure in his dream.

But what is that? The teddy moves and kisses him. As he does so, he has a very wet nose, which he presses into Matt's face.

He opens his eyes and sees a small black and white dog with thick curly fur. He wags his tail and licks him lovingly across his face.

Matt pushes him away and sits up, but the baby dog jumps right back into his arms and snuggles in. He pushes him away again and looks at him. He doesn't look dangerous at all.

Carefully, Matt touches the soft fur and strokes him with his fingertips. The little dog throws himself on his back and holds out his belly for him to scratch.

A little girl climbs into the garden through a hole in the fence. She calls out, "Fluffy, Fluffy," and runs toward Matt.

The girl looks pretty relieved to have found her little dog again. Without saying anything to Matt, she takes Fluffy in her arms and runs home with him. Matt looks after the two, not excited at all. On the contrary, he feels good.

Later, Matt talks to his mom about the little dog's visit.

She tells him how proud she is of him because he overcame his fear today. He had a real animal experience to help him to conquer his groundless fear of all animals.

That was brave. Matt thinks again about what he has discussed with his mom when he is already in bed.

Having courage doesn't mean deliberately putting yourself in danger. And being afraid is not always bad.

It is sometimes necessary because it protects him from danger.

But it needs a real reason. Matt understands

what his mother means and wonders if practicing being brave is possible.

Matt thinks it would be nice if the little dog revisited him. Then he falls asleep right away.

COURAGE: CHAPTER 2

WHAT DOES LOVE FEEL LIKE?

That was not good what Basti's best friend Thea said to him. Before he understood it, he already felt a grumbling in his stomach. So, he didn't answer anything when Thea ran away.

Basti has known Thea since he can remember. Even their strollers had always stood next to each other in the garden, back when they were still babies.

Thea is only three months older than Basti. Her parents lived in the same house as Basti's family.

Unlike Thea, Basti has a big brother. On paper, his name is Lorenz, after his grandpa. But because that sounds so old-fashioned, no one has ever called him that. Even the teachers call him Renzo, just like everyone else.

When Basti can't remember something from the past, he asks his brother. Sometimes Renzo makes fun of Basti and tells him crap. But it's true about Thea. They could almost be twins.

Even though Thea's parents later built a house and moved away. Fortunately, the kindergarten they shared was in the middle.

Now they go to the same school. Maybe it's just

good that they're at least in different classes.

Thea is Basti's trusted confidant. She knows everything about him, more than his mother and more than Renzo. He's about to turn fourteen and is in a funny mood. Basti is not the only one who thinks this way.

What she doesn't know is how much Basti admires her. She's the best player on the handball team, and when he doesn't understand math problems, Thea can explain them to him immediately.

She then says he should listen in class instead of nonsense, so he'll get it.

Basti likes that about her. She never brags about something she can do better.

But he's also good at sometimes fooling around with her or being crazy. And best of all, Thea never says anything to anyone. Never!

Not when he hid Magnus' smartphone in the toilet, wrapped in toilet paper because he kept taking stupid pictures of Basti; not even when he decorated the substitute teacher's scooter with crazy stickers. And not when he climbed out of the window at night to take part in some stupid test of courage. Who dares to swim in the dark in Dennis' father's fish pond? Afterward, he thought it was pretty dumb himself.

When his mother tries to question Thea after he's done something wrong, she usually says, "Ask Basti yourself."

As I said, Thea doesn't snitch. That's cool. Thea is the very best buddy he can imagine. And if he had a sister, she would have to be just like her.

But for a few days now, everything has been mixed up. All of a sudden, on the way home from school, she kissed him on the mouth.

Then she said she wanted Basti to be her boyfriend because she was in love with him.

Basti didn't say anything. And now he is avoiding Thea. Sometimes he thinks, yeah, sure, she's my best friend, and the next moment he believes that feels wrong. And sometimes, all his thoughts are mixed up, and he doesn't know what to think anymore.

He misses Thea after two days; ideally, they don't go to the same class. Basti is careful that they don't run into each other on the way to school or during breaks.

Instead of going out into the courtyard, he prefers to spend the break inside, starting his homework.

Tomorrow is finally Saturday, and he has time on the weekend to think about all of this. Maybe he feels terrible.

Typically, Basti spends the weekend with his family. But this weekend, everything is a little different. Aunt Nora, Basti's mom's sister, is coming to visit.

His mom hasn't seen her for a long time. She wants to spend as much time as possible with her.

She has suggested going to the big animal park in the forest together.

Basti likes to go there and especially loves the moose with their slobbery mouths.

His dad won't be coming along. He has a tennis tournament and therefore only has time in the evening. And Renzo doesn't feel like going, he says. As always lately.

“Have you already made a date with Thea for the weekend?” asks Basti’s mom at lunch.

“She could come to the wild animal park with us tomorrow. Why don’t you give her a call right now?”

Even though he’s full, Basti gets another filled pancake. He doesn’t need to answer if he has something in his mouth.

His mom has another explanation: “You’re really hungry today. You’re probably growing again, making the next push.”

Renzo grins stupidly. That’s supposed to mean he sees through it. Behind her mother’s back, Basti grimaces at him.

That’s supposed to mean I don’t believe anything you say. Basti hopes that when Aunt Nora comes tomorrow morning, his mother will have forgotten all about Thea.

But she didn’t!

When Basti comes into the kitchen for breakfast on Saturday morning, the first thing she asks him is, “So, does Thea feel like coming along?”

Basti quickly turns away because he feels himself blushing. He doesn't want to lie to his mom, but he can't tell her what happened after all.

He pretends he didn't hear her and pours milk over his cereal. That's no solution, either. So, he shakes his head without looking at her.

"Are you having an argument with Thea?" she asks.

Basti makes a throwing-away motion. He puts his empty cereal bowl in the sink.

"I'm going to pack up my stuff for the trip tomorrow."

Already he's out of the kitchen. Luckily, Aunt Nora meets him on the stairs. She'll distract his mom. She is still sleepy and smiles at him.

The trip was not as much fun as Basti had hoped. His mom and Aunt Nora talk the whole time and don't care about him. They haven't seen each other for a long time. Sure, they want to talk to each other!

But also, the weather is gloomy. And not even the moose show up. Only one is standing at the edge of the forest, much too small to see.

Basti is disappointed. The only hope is the miniature goats, which Basti lures with the food bought at the entrance to feed and pet them.

It would have been more fun with Thea and Basti angrily kicking a fence and scaring a few ducks.

He can't get his problem with Thea out of his head. There is no girl in the world that Basti likes better than her. But at barely eleven, he doesn't want to "go" with a girl yet.

When Aunt Nora leaves the next day, his mom enters Basti's room. He is lying on the bed and listening to music.

His dad is not yet back from tennis, and Renzo is out with friends. They are alone in the house.

Before she says anything, Basti knows his mom wants to talk to him. She sits down on the edge of the bed. Basti takes off his headphones but says nothing. He waits for his mom to start talking.

"You're not just disappointed that it wasn't so great for you at the park."

Basti shakes his head and looks at the ceiling.

"Do you want to talk?" his mom asks.

Basti shrugs his shoulders. He doesn't.

"What about Thea? I can see perfectly well that there's something wrong between you two. You didn't even ask her if she wanted to go to the animal park with us, did you?"

His mom carefully takes Basti's hand and strokes it.

"Don't you want to tell me? Maybe I can help you. And what you say will definitely stay between us, too. You know that."

Out of the blue, Basti starts to sniffle. The tears roll down his face without him being able to do anything about it. How can he talk to Mama without telling Thea? He wants some advice, but ... how?

Basti's mom takes him in her arms and comforts him. When Basti has calmed down, he wipes his eyes with his sleeve and sits up.

"I'd like to tell you, but I can't. Because of Thea. I don't know if I'd give her away if I told you what she said."

"Was it that bad?"

Basti nods.

His mom thinks for a moment before making a suggestion.

“You can just tell me about yourself. What you’d like to say to her or what you’d like to do to make things right between you.”

“And then what if she doesn’t talk to me at all when I tell her what I think?” he asked.

“Basti, Thea has always been your best friend. You’re almost like twins. She’s the sister you don’t have. I can’t imagine that your inseparable friendship can break so easily.”

“Everyone has to be able to put up with a different opinion from their friend sometimes.”

“And what if I don’t talk to her and wait until she forgets?” Basti squints his eyes as if that might make him wish for that easy solution.

“Basti, that would be dishonest and cowardly. Thea deserves that you be honest with her, doesn’t she? Or would you want something else from her?”

Basti reacts indignantly at the idea: “No! She should always tell me what she thinks.”

“And I guess she did that now, and you didn’t

like it. If you're brave, you'll tell her what you didn't like about it."

Basti's mom strokes his head one more time and then gets up.

"Good night, sweetheart!"

"Sleep well, Mommy! ..., thank you!"

Monday comes. Basti has the grumbling in his stomach again. He can't pay attention in class because he keeps thinking about what he wants to say to Thea.

He has decided to wait for her on the way home. He hopes she will walk the last part from the bus stop alone. That's why he rode his bike all the way home today.

Basti leans against a house wall so that Thea doesn't see him from afar. There she comes. He recognizes her by her energetic pace.

Thea takes pretty big steps for a girl. Today she doesn't look ahead but pensively at the ground. She could not have seen Basti and was startled when he suddenly stood before her.

Embarrassed, they stand in front of each other. Basti takes a deep breath before he speaks. What he wants to say to her now takes a lot of courage.

“Hi Thea! Shall we walk together to your place?”

Thea smiles weakly. Basti walks on Thea’s right side, so his bike is between them.

“Thea? I want everything to be like before,” Basti starts carefully. His voice sounds all croaky because he’s so nervous.

“Me too,” Thea whispers.

“You know, we’re not even eleven yet ...”

“I just turned eleven, have you forgotten?” replies Thea defiantly.

“No, I haven’t! And I don’t want to have a girlfriend yet!” Now it’s out, and Basti exhales the air he’s been holding in excitement. Before Thea can confuse him with an answer, he quickly continues talking.

“And besides, you’re way too important to me to have you as a girlfriend yet. We are too young. You’ve always been my best friend. I wish it would always stay that way. Always. Because you're the only person I can tell anything to and do anything with. And being like a couple is just something else, I think. Renzo already went out with a girl on a date. Now they can't stand each other. I always want to like you, though."

Basti has stopped and looks at Thea questioningly. She keeps walking, and Basti runs to catch up to her.

"What if I ever fall in love with another boy?" "I think that's okay, as long as you still have time for me too and we stay friends."

"Really?"

"I guess."

"That was pretty brave of you to tell me. I was afraid you'd always hide from me now."

"That would be stupid. Who would I talk to then?"

"Come on, let's go to the water and look at the ships!" Thea goes around Basti to the other side and hangs on to him.

Basti's young heart is deeply touched.

JOIN THE KROKO PUBLISHING NEWSLETTER TODAY - YOUR TICKET TO A WORLD OF CHILDREN'S BOOKS!

Hey there! Are you a book lover, especially when it comes to children's books? Then you've come to the right place! Join the Kroko Publishing newsletter today and stay up to date with the latest children's book adventures. Be the first to know about our new releases, special offers, exciting promotions, and more.

Don't wait - scan the QR code or enter the URL in your browser and join our family of kroko fans today.

https://kroko-verlag.com/newsletter/

IMPRINT

Original edition
First edition 2022

Cover design: Danileoart, www.danileoart.com
Typesetting and layout: Danileoart